Dear Paula,
you've got what i
takes — faith & a
umor — Now, that's...
With lo
Linette

Now, *That's* A Miracle!

Reflections On
Faith And Life

Richard Stoll Armstrong

Illustrations by
Bil Canfield

CSS Publishing Company, Inc., Lima, Ohio

NOW, *THAT'S* A MIRACLE!

Copyright ©1996 by
CSS Publishing Company, Inc.
Lima, Ohio

Some scripture quotations are from the *Revised Standard Version of the Bible*, copyrighted 1946, 1952 (c), 1971, 1973, by the Division of Christian Education of the National Council of the Churches of Christ in the USA. Used by permission.

Some scripture quotations are from the *New Revised Standard Version of the Bible*, copyright 1989 by the Division of Christian Education of the National Council of the Churches of Christ in the USA. Used by permission.

Library of Congress Cataloging-in-Publication Data

Armstrong, Richard Stoll, 1924-
    Now, that's a miracle! : reflections on faith and life / Richard Stoll Armstrong ; illustrations by Bil Canfiled.
        p.   cm.
    Includes bibliographical references (p.) and indexes.
    ISBN 0-7880-0762-9
    1. Christian poetry, American. I. Title.
PS3551.R5S PS3551.4765N69   1996
811'.54—dc20   96-7630
                                                                    CIP

ISBN: 0-7880-0762-9   PRINTED IN U.S.A.

Table Of Contents

Page

Preface

This volume of poetry has been long in the making, its contents having been written over a period of many years. As was the case with my earlier poetry book, *Enough, Already!*, the publication of this collection is in response to the urging of pastors and lay persons who have heard one or more of the rhymes in various settings.

The reader should understand that many of the verses were written for use in sermons or talks. Thus they are suitable to be spoken, with a message that the hearers can understand and relate to. Whereas *Enough, Already!* is a most humorous commentary on life in the church, the poems in this volume are of a more serious nature. The contents, as the subtitle suggests, are my reflections on matters of faith and life, covering a wide gamut of topics, with no unifying theme intended. Most of these poems were inspired by or related to, though they were not intended to be expositions of, biblical texts. These are footnoted for the convenience of those who may wish to use the poems in connection with those particular texts.

The usefulness of the rhymes is not limited to the original context, of course, and I hope pastors and others will find them helpful as illustrative material for the pulpit or the classroom, or as a resource for their personal devotional or relaxed reading. To facilitate the retrieval process I have provided a topical index, which should aid those who may want to use some of the poems, or parts of poems, in the pulpit or the classroom, or in their church bulletin or newsletter. There is also an index of first lines.

Many of the texts could be set to music, and tunes have already been composed to some of them (e.g., "An Ordination Prayer," "Faith, Hope, and Love," and "Who Builds the House"). This is a project yet to be completed, and I would welcome the opportunity to work with a compatible composer on these and other texts that I have written.

Almost all of the poems in this collection are rhymes, although they represent a variety of poetic meter and structure. "Do You

Really Believe?" is one of the few unrhymed poems. Its poetic feature is the consistent employment of ten-syllable lines. "Christianity Is. . ." is another unrhymed poem, with a unique graphic structure. "The Story Briefly Told," "The Calling Cycle," and "Relevant Clichés" also have various structural symmetries.

The birth of some of the poems took place over a period of months and sometimes even years, while other verses resulted from moments of sudden inspiration. Regardless of the length of the gestation period, every one of these rhymes was a labor of love, and each one has its own message or purpose.

I am deeply indebted to my good friend Bil Canfield, whose sensitive illustrations help bring the poems to life. What a privilege and pleasure it has been to work with such a talented artist on this and my previous volume of poetry. I marvel at his ability to portray graphically what I am attempting to express in rhyme. I look forward to our continuing collaboration in the future.

I also wish to express my deep gratitude to the many persons who have heard and responded to some of these poems over the years, including friends and family members with whom I shared them in more intimate settings. Once again the person whose comments and suggestions have been the most helpful is my wife Margie, who always understands better than anyone else what it is I am trying to say, and without whose encouragement and support my poetry would probably never have been published.

Richard Stoll Armstrong
Princeton, New Jersey

To my mother,
Elsie Stoll Armstrong,
a poetic soul,
who did not live to see or hear
many of these poems,
but who from my childhood
appreciated and encouraged
the poetic spirit in me.

Now, *That's* A Miracle![1]

Of all the miracles I've known

the greatest one must be

that God in Jesus Christ can love

the likes of you and me!

Called To Freedom[2]

You were called to freedom. . .

    freedom from the worship of the idol of success;
    freedom from the bondage of the passion to possess;
    freedom from the conscience-binding pressure to conform;
    freedom from the selfish will's resistance to reform;
    freedom to embrace the truth, when others would deny it;
    freedom to defend the right, when others would defy it;
    freedom to be humble, when the world would make you
        proud;
    freedom to go God's way, caring not to please the crowd.

And the truth will make you free...

    free to be a servant and yet call none other master;
    free to trust God's gracious will in triumph or disaster;
    free to love your enemies and pray for those who curse
        you;
    free to give without expecting life to reimburse you;
    free, persuaded naught can separate you from God's love;
    free, empowered by God's grace and wisdom from above;
    free, believing God can work for good in everything;
    free! — more than a conqueror, through Jesus Christ the
        King!

A Friendship Prayer[3]

Give me a friend, O God —
>   not one who makes me feel I'm right, whenever I am wrong,
>   confirms me in my prejudice and pushes me along
>   the always easy pathways of my self-deceiving sin,
>   where good intentions quickly die and conscience soon wears
>   thin.

I need a friend, O God —
>   not one who flatters me with praise I know I don't deserve,
>   or when I need to hear the truth, declines for lack of nerve,
>   and tells me just what others think is music to my ears,
>   condoning or excusing all my failures, faults, and fears.

I want a friend, O God —
>   whose love for me demands I take the higher, harder way
>   and calls me to confess my guilt, whatever price I pay.
>   Far better that I choose to live with honor in defeat,
>   than bask in fame and glory gained by falsehood and deceit.

I have a friend, O God —
>   who wants my best, inspires my best, accepts no less from
>   me,
>   who sets me an example I can follow earnestly,
>   expecting me to stand for truth and goodness, come what may,
>   and judging me by what I do and not just what I say.

You are that friend, O God —
> a friend whose love is life itself, whose truth has set me free,
> who sees not only what I am but what I long to be,
> who knows my every weakness yet forgives the wrongs I've
>> done.
> Such friendship is for all to share, through Jesus Christ, your
>> Son.

Incident At Nazareth[4]

He came one day to Nazareth, where he had been brought up,
   and went into the synagogue by custom. He stood up
to read. They handed him a book — Isaiah's book. He knew
   what they should hear. He found the place and read it
       through:
"The Spirit of the Lord," he said, "is on me. I have been
   anointed to proclaim good news. . ." They seemed to take it in.
"Release to captives; to the blind, recovery of sight;
   and liberty to those oppressed by poverty or might."
He closed the book and took his seat, all eyes on him intent.
   Today this scripture is fulfilled!" They nodded their assent,
and wondered at his gracious words. Was this not Joseph's son?
   But soon their favor turned, when he went on to say that none
of them could claim to be by right among the Lord's elect,
   for God was free to choose or save those whom *they* would
       reject.
"No prophet is acceptable in his own land," he said.
   "The Lord may pass his people by, and bless someone instead
like Zarephath, the Sidonite, to whom Elijah went.
   To Naaman the Syrian, the prophet, too, was sent."

The synagogue was filled with wrath. "Who does he think he is?
 — this carpenter!" They led him out. They were no
     friends of his!
They marched him to a nearby cliff and would have thrown him
     down,
   but passing through the midst of them, he left his own home
     town.

Caution On Causes

It's good when your heart has been gripped by a cause
       that calls for devotion and zeal.
But if your cause blinds you to God's higher laws,
       how can you to God then appeal?

When cause without conscience gives purpose its prod
       and on the expedient leans,
The question remains for the servant of God:
       Are ends justified by the means?

No matter how worthy the cause you espouse,
       no matter how noble the goal,
If gaining that end is the first of your vows,
       beware, lest you mortgage your soul!

18

Race And The Race[5]

Defining identity strictly by race

     denies that in Christ all are one.

For God does not look at the skin on your face;

     God judges the race you have run.

Hard To Swallow[6]

Behold, you scoffers, and wonder and perish.
       The Lord does a deed in your days,
a deed you will never believe, when they tell you
       a Savior from death God did raise.

This word from Paul and the prophet Habakkuk
       gives pause to our confident claim
that we would not have resisted, as some did
       in Paul's day, nor acted the same.

So, too, their forebears did wonder and marvel,
       nor could their cold hearts take it in
that God had decided to rouse the Chaldeans —
       a judgment on Israel's sin!

To fight the truth is our sad inclination,
       whenever a cross is involved;
for when our own heart has been hardened against it,
       by grace must our doubt be resolved.

Wrestling With Sin[7]

Why can't I do the good I want,
      the things I know I should?
Why do I always do the things
      I hate and not the good?

Why is it I can know what's right,
      and yet my will complies
not with the good I know, but with
      the sin that in me lies?

O wretched me! Who can relieve
      my soul from this discord?
My faith cries out, "Thanks be to God,
      through Jesus Christ our Lord!"

A Helping Hand[8]

O Christ, had I one wish I fain would be
　　　　the one who bore your cross to Calvary,
who walked beside you on the dusty way
　　　　and shared the pain you bore for me that day.

If only it were my hand that you clasped,
　　　　my shoulder which your aching fingers grasped,
Then would I dare to face that painful scene,
　　　　if it were I upon whom you could lean.

But, Jesus, you are walking even yet,
　　　　your cross upon your back. Need I regret,
as if all opportunity were gone?
　　　　The road to Calvary goes on and on!

Beneath another's cross your face I see.
　　　　My neighbor's burden is your cross for me.
Your silent sorrow bids me understand
　　　　that you will always need a helping hand.

A Christmas Prayer[9]

God give us grace. . .

To see

>   beyond the gleam and glitter
>   of our tinseled trees
>   a dim lit stable
>   not at all like these,

To hear

>   above the clash and clamor
>   of the market throng
>   an angel's call for peace
>   in silent song,

To feel

>   in all the merry madness
>   of our festive cheer
>   the Savior's presence
>   in our hearts this year.

The Story Briefly Told[10]

A weary, wayward world —
>*In the beginning was the Word. . .*
>>*and the Word was God.*

A star among the stars —
>*The true light that enlightens everyone*
>>*was coming into the world.*

A new-born baby's cry —
>*And the Word became flesh and dwelt among us*
>>*full of grace and truth.*

A man upon a cross —
>*He was in the world. . .*
>>*yet the world knew him not.*

An empty tomb —
>*But to all who received him . . .*
>>*he gave power to become children of God.*

Christianity Is . . .

not a philosophy
  to be discussed
but a message
  to be proclaimed,
   which calls
not for comment
  about an idea
but for commitment
  to a cause
   and demands
not correct conclusions
  about a book
but complete confidence
  in a Person
   whose

life,

death,

resurrection, ascension,

and

living

presence

are

not a subject

     to be explained

but a faith

     to be affirmed.

The Real Me[11]

God created me. I don't understand —
       is what I am now the "me" that God planned?
If by the Lord's grace I am what I am,
       can I be to blame, whatever I am?

Is claiming that just a pretext to say
       whatever I am is really okay?
As if what I am is not up to me?
       So blame it on God, and I go scot-free!

Or does God alone observe the real me,
       not just what I am, but what I can be?
God knows my desires as well as my needs.
       God knows the intent behind all my deeds.

The "me" others know is not the real me;
       nor is it the "me" I want them to see.
I'm not what I seem. Yet is it not true,
       that masquerade "me" is part of me, too?

Beneath the facades the world need not see;
　　the masks that I choose reveal the real me!
Indeed, I confess that it may well be
　　those phoney facades are closest to me.

To know who I am may be but a sham.
　　Salvation is this: to know *whose* I am.
To know I am Christ's by grace and that he
　　can free me through faith to be the real me.

Even His Brothers[12]

Whenever your faith takes a tumble
  and you're caught in the clutches of doubt,
whenever you falter or stumble
  and you can't seem to figure things out,
when you're not quite so sure as some others
  that the Christ really died to save you,
just remember that even his brothers
  were averse to believe in him, too.

Even they sought a sign of his power,
  and they couldn't at first comprehend,
when he said that it wasn't his hour.
  But they also believed in the end.
Overcoming their doubt and their sadness
  they all met in that famed upper room,
and the pathway from sorrow to gladness
  was the road from the cross to the tomb.

The Creative Word[13]

God's word is God's creative act,
        effecting weal or woe.
To bring from naught the things that are
        God spoke and it was so!

Before the earth was ever formed
        God said, "Let there be light,"
and there was light! God called it Day;
        God called the darkness Night.

"And let there be a firmament,"
        God said, "and let there be
a sun, and moon, and stars above,
        the sky, the land, the sea.

"Let there be plants and living things
        and man and woman, too" —
six days of work, and then a day
        of rest, when God was through.

God saw that what was made was good,
        including humankind,
For God's creative word and act
        are one in God's own mind.

A Christmas Song[14]

I don't know what the shepherds heard
    that night so long ago.
Angelic messengers of God
    defy my mind, although
I love to hear the story of
    the angels from on high,
and sing about that holy night
    when music filled the sky.

For if we hear the angel song
    and know the joy it brings,
then Christian faith today as then
    must be a faith that sings!
A song there is for all to sing,
    yet each one's own must write —
a song of faith and hope and love,
    a song of truth and light.

Have we a Christmas Song, I ask,
    a message to proclaim?
What news have we to share with those
    who may not know the name
of him whose birth we celebrate
    each year on Christmas day?
Is there a melody of works
    that blends with what we say?

The shepherds heard the angels' song
       with gladness and good cheer.
I wonder if our Christmas Song
       brings joy to those who hear,
and hope to those who have no hope
       and need a helping hand?
A song of acts our song must be,
       before they'll understand.

The Christ of whom the angels sang,
   a servant Christ was he,
and if we want to be like him
   then servants we must be —
our Christmas Song, a servant song;
   our gospel backed by deeds;
our peace on earth, good will to all;
   its theme: our neighbors' needs.

What better way to tell the news
   about the Savior's birth?
How better to proclaim good will
   and peace to all on earth?
So let our hearts and voices now
   blend with the angel throng,
for what would "Merry Christmas!" mean
   without a Christmas Song?

My call to be a minister I never will forget.
> In retrospect I know my faith was not Christ-centered yet.
I spoke not of a "call of Christ" nor thought about it much;
>> I should have been quite mystified, were it described as
>> such.

A personal relationship with Christ I couldn't claim,
>> and it was even hard for me to pray in Jesus' name.
It truly was a call of God; there's no doubt in my mind,
>> but putting it in terms of Christ — those words I could not
>> find.

I came to know the living Lord on seminary sod,
>> and now my faith in Jesus Christ informs my faith in God.
From God to Christ, from Christ to God, thus with the Spirit's
aid
>> by providential grace was my Christology delayed.

Relevant Clichés

How will I know the truth?
But where do I find it?
Is the Bible God's word?
Can it be understood?
Will I have any doubts?
Can I prove there's a God?
Then my faith is a gift?
Will God give me that gift?
What if I should say No?
Does God care about me?
Where does Jesus fit in?
So is Jesus the Christ?
Thus the gospel is Christ?
How do I accept Christ?
Will it cost me a lot?
Will it mean sacrifice?
Will my life be the same?
What if I sin again?
Should I give my life now?
I have seen the true light!

It's yours for the asking!
It is in the Good Book!
You better believe it!
You gotta have faith!
There's no doubt about it!
You can't prove it by me!
You can thank God for that!
You can take it or leave it!
Then you haven't a prayer!
You can bet your sweet life!
Have I got news for you!
It's the gospel truth!
That's what it's all about!
Stand up and be counted!
What have you got to lose?
You can't take it with you!
That's for you to decide!
It would be no surprise!
The sooner the better!
It's a sight for sore eyes!

Convocation Day[16]

Are these my thoughts, or are they dreams?
The voice is real,
and yet I feel
beyond the reach of any well-intended word
I may have heard
but did not really hear.
So near
the vocal sound, and yet so far
from my half-conscious mind, it seems.
My mental door is left ajar,
as in a stupor, vaguely sensing all
yet feeling not at all.
My dry, unblinking eyes are seeing naught,
as though they have been caught
in some weird state of flux between
reality
and fantasy,
while I am bound
with chains unseen
by those around,
who, far from mean,
are quite transfixed by words addressed
to them, but nonetheless expressed
in unfeigned sympathy
for me,
because our son has died
this very morn — their convocation day.
Why am I sitting here this way?
Because, resolved
to be involved,
I forced myself at last to come.
My body, mind and soul are numb.

I have not cried
as yet. I feel as if I'm in a kind of trance,
aware enough to dare to hope by some divinely ordained chance
that this indeed is one nightmare
from which I shall awake
to find our son still there.
But my heartache
is much too strong,
though all along
his mom and I have known this day
would come.
Still we had hoped by some
much prayed-for miracle of grace
that God would spare our son,
whose face
is in my mind's eye clearly now.
The speaker's voice announces how
"One of our students and his wife today
have suffered a great loss,"
and something else about a cross.
Then, for some reason, suddenly
I'm jolted from my reverie
by my harsh rediscovery
that all these words of sympathy
are meant for Margie and for me.
It is *our* son whose death is news
to all the strangers in these pews.
The voice confirms my saddest fears,
and now I'm fighting back the tears.
The muscles of my throat are sore
from swallowing the lump. What's more,
I feel a claustrophobic urge
to rush out from this crowded place.
I'm on the verge
of screaming, No!

It can't be so.
I can't erase
the awful truth, and yet. . .
and yet
there's still a shade
of disbelief that will not fade,
nor will it let
me rest at ease until I know.
Is it false hope, or morbid fear,
or grief compelling me to go?
The friendly greetings that I hear,
as I push through the parting crowd,
are answered with a weak, forced smile,
but not aloud. And all the while
my heart pounds with anticipation,
not in hopeful expectation.
It is as if some heartless fiend
has gleaned
a devilish delight
in tempting me
to think tonight
that Ricky might be there,
and thus propelling me
by hope that soon would turn into a deep despair,
a cruel trick, the kind
a sadist plays upon a tortured mind.
The tempo of my heartbeat
now is faster than my running feet,
crossing the lawn, as I have done
so many times to see my son.
Then bounding up the concrete stair
and pushing wide the door, I stare
into the darkness of the room,
where normally there is a light.
But not tonight,

for Margie is exhausted by her long ordeal.
She did not feel
that she could go with me
to such a convocation.
Having had to bear the brunt of Ricky's recent tribulation,
she has gone for days
and days
with very little sleep or rest,
and both of us had thought it best
that she stay home instead.
Since she is now in bed,
I gently close the door,
and then, I do the same
as I have done so many times before:
I softly call his name.
It's not that I
think he'll reply,
but that I must now play again
the little game
we played, we two,
which in the final days I knew
would have to come to this,
a sad pretending, like a lover's kiss
bestowed upon the breeze,
to sadden, not to please
the heart,
which, though about to break,
must from the start
indulge its pain
for love's sake.
So I wait in vain,
suspended in the silent void,
to hear once more the bravely cheerful voice of one
I so enjoyed
and loved, reply

"Hi, Daddy!" to be followed by
my "hello hug." But now
I feel the agonizing absence. Yet somehow
I cannot let myself believe our little boy is gone.
My loving wife will comfort me
and I her, and we both will see
that life goes on,
as people say,
and convocations like today,
while she and I,
so painfully bereft
are left
to wonder, Why?

Contagious Faith?

There's a popular apothegm going around,
       that too many a Christian has bought.
On the surface the saying seems perfectly sound:
       "Faith in Christ is not taught; it is caught!"

What a clever remark! That's the right emphasis!
       It's a saw one can swallow with ease.
But if faith is contagious, my question is this:
       Why don't more people have the disease?

There once was a man in the land of Uz,
>as righteous a man as there ever was.
Renowned for his faith and his wealth was he.
>He prayed every day for his family.
Now, Job was the name of this blameless man,
>whose life was a breeze till his woes began,
when Satan appeared on the scene one day
>from roaming the earth to and fro for prey.
"Consider my true servant Job," said God.
>But Satan replied, "You have spared the rod.
The work of Job's hands you have blessed by grace.
>Just take what he has and he'll curse your face."
So God tested Job just to prove his worth.
>Has anyone suffered like Job on earth?
He lost all his children, his help, his wealth.
>But Satan was told not to take Job's health.
"Consider my servant," said God again.
>"He kept his integrity even when
you took all he had." Satan then replied,
>"Touch skin, flesh and bone and you'll be denied.
All that he now has he will give for life."
>"Curse God, and go die," said his forlorn wife.
Despite all his troubles Job did not sin.
>And that's where the problem for us comes in:
The question of evil and good, you know,
>is, Why should a good person suffer so?
Job's friends tried to answer to no avail,
>and all of our efforts are doomed to fail.

The lesson Job teaches is How, not Why.

     To cope with our troubles until we die
is much more important to understand
     and surely much closer to what God planned
for us to derive from the Book of Job,
     than doctrines of evil for us to probe.
What help would it be, even if we could?
     We know that in all things God works for good
with those who love God. That's our hope always,
     and so we can give God our grateful praise.

Hope For The Future[18]

It is said that the future belongs to the young,
      but that saying is simply not true.
That's because when the bell of the future has rung,
      that day's young will be somebody new.

Why does each generation repeat that cliché,
      as if it were something profound?
For will not tomorrow be always today
      to those who will still be around?

Furthermore, there's no comfort at all in the thought
      that the future belongs to the young.
For we are the future for those who once thought
      that the hope of the world on *us* hung!

Though I know what they mean when they say what they say,
      such a word from believers is odd.
For what hope for the world is there really today,
      if the future belongs not to God?

Appreciation Ratio[19]

Ten lepers Jesus healed one day, but only one returned
   to thank him, and because of that another blessing earned.
We tend to think that one came back to thank the Lord is fine,
   but Jesus said, "Were not ten cleansed? Where are the other
   nine?"
Among the blessings God bestows there's one I recommend.
   Appreciation is a gift of God, I do contend.
Just think about it, and you'll see exactly why I say,
   appreciation is a gift God gives to give away.
How few there are who bother to express their gratitude.
   Their failure to give thanks reflects a thoughtless
   attitude.
Why, hardly anyone these days will take the time to write.
   Folks act as if each favor they receive is theirs by right.
The people who express their thanks give other folks a lift,
   and that is why I view appreciation as a gift,
that one both has and also gives, as faithful stewards do.
   So when God's gifts you're listing, add "appreciation," too.

Second Fiddle[20]

From John the Baptist we could learn about humility.
    He testified that Jesus was a greater man than he.
"There comes one after me," he said, "far mightier than I,
    whose shoestrings I am not worthy to stoop down and
    untie."
John could have thought of Jesus as a threat to his renown,
    a rival prophet on the rise, while he was going down.
Indeed, John did confess that, when he said, "He must increase!"
    And still without the least regret, he said, "I must decrease!"
Hats off to those who play the role that John the Baptist played
    without resentment or ill will, when on them it is laid.

Tempted As We Are?[21]

Whenever we are tempted, even though we don't give in,
  is not the base desire itself a subtle form of sin?
If Jesus had no urges for a woman sexually,
  then was he really tempted at all points like you and me?
If Jesus *had* those feelings tempting him from deep within,
  how can we say that he was just like us, yet without sin?
Now, that's another paradox that I have thought about
  for years, and one that I admit I haven't figured out.

The Calling Cycle

The God who calls is
the God who guides is
the God who provides is
the God who enables is
the God who calls. . .

In His Steps[22]

One who follows Jesus should be careful where one sprints.
To follow in Christ's footsteps doesn't mean in his footprints!
>   We are called to follow him
>   in *our* world, not in his.
One who follows Jesus this perspective should not lose:
Following in Jesus' steps does not mean in his shoes!
>   We are called to be like Christ
>   not to be Christ.
One who follows Jesus Christ should never be misled:
Following in Jesus' steps does not mean in his stead!
>   We are called to represent him
>   not to replace him.

The Law Of Perversity[23]

Why do things always happen just when I don't want them to?
Why do I always do the thing I didn't want to do?
Why do the good things always stop before I've had my turn?
Why am I always tested on the part I didn't learn?
Why am I always overheard the times my tongue has slipped?
Why is it people always spot the numbers I have skipped?
Why is it I can't get away with risks that others take?
Why am I always caught for the one error that I make?
Why do I have the feeling Fate must have it in for me?
I am the victim of a law: it's called "perversity."

It's easy for most anyone at times to feel this way.
Saint Paul himself was wrestling with this problem in his day.
"I do not do the good I want," confessed Paul honestly.
"The evil that I do not want is what I do — poor me!"
And then he asked "Who'll rescue me from such a wretched
    state?
Thanks be to God through Jesus Christ our Lord!" — our
    advocate!
There is the answer to the problem of perversity.
By grace through faith in Jesus Christ we're "superstition-free"!

53

Infinite Flexibility[24]

In everything God works for good with those who seek God's will.
    I learned that lesson long ago, and I believe it still.
For many years I tried to name this holy attribute.
    I searched for words that might express my thoughts, but none would suit.
God's mercy, power, grace, compassion, wisdom, truth, or love?
    The concept I was searching for was none of the above.
It had to do with all of them and yet was something more.
    I wondered why it had not been identified before.
At last I hit upon a term which says it all for me.
    It has to do with what I call God's "flexibility."
What if two Christians, both sincere, pray for opposing things?
    How can the God they pray to grant the prayer that each one brings?
What if two enemies at war both thinking their cause just,
    should pray to God for victory in equal faith and trust?
What if while golfers pray for sun, the farmers pray for rain?
    How God could meet the needs of both was once hard to explain,
but now I know this problem was not God's at all but mine.
    If God is God there is no way we can God's will confine.
For God can work within a billion lives at once for good.
    God's *infinitely* flexible! If that is understood,
then one can see how things can work according to God's will,
    yet every human being's free to choose for good or ill.
The unbelieving world can't comprehend this truth at all.
    "*We* know that all things work for good" — we who *believe*, said Paul.
So God can work in everything in such a wondrous way
    that everyone will know through faith God honors what we pray.
In suffering and sorrow, yes, and even in our sin,
    our God can work for good with those who seek God's will therein.

What greater confirmation can there be for what I've said
    than what God did for us in raising Jesus from the dead?
For sin nailed Jesus to the cross, and yet through faith we see
    that out of that defeat God brought eternal victory.

Secret Sins 25

There are blotches on my character that everybody sees.

I have obvious shortcomings, but my problem isn't these.

No, my problem is my *secret* sins, about which no one knows.

I say no one, but I know that God is well aware of those.

When I'm criticized unjustly and I start to moan and groan,

I just wonder what they'd say if all my secret sins were known.

Then I'm thankful for God's mercy and true penitence begins,

when I realize God loves me — yes, despite my secret sins!

A Christmas Wish

My wish for the world every Christmas would be
    three beautiful gifts that no money can buy.
Most precious they are, and yet perfectly free
    to those who believe the good news from on high.
They're not to be wasted or hoarded, but shared
    with others, so they can then share the gifts, too,
for these are the gifts of a God who has cared
    enough to have offered them to me and you:
The faith of the shepherds who looked at the sky,
    the hope of the Magi who followed the star,
the love of a mother for one who would die
    for all the world's sin on a wooden crossbar.

This I Know[26]

I know that one's faith is a gift of the Lord
    and that gift has been given to me.
I know that the Lord I believe in has poured
    out his mercy and grace upon me.

I know I was called by a God who is real
    to a brand new vocational start.
I know I am loved by a God who can heal
    all the pain of a once broken heart.

I know I'm forgiven by One who can see
    every fault, and shortcoming, and sin,
and yet who has deigned to use someone like me
    to bear witness to Jesus therein.

I know that in everything God works for good,
    for God always has done so with me.
I know without Jesus that I never could
    have found out what it means to be free.

I know God has guided me all of the way,
    and the Spirit is working in me.
I know that because of Christ now I can say,
    "I was blind once, but now I can see!"

A Prayer For Today[27]

Help me a loving life to live
    today, O Lord, today.
May I forgive as you forgive,
    today, O Lord, today.

Cleanse me of my unworthiness
    today, O Lord, today,
and rid my heart of bitterness,
    today, O Lord, today.

Remove my selfishness and pride,
    today, O Lord, today,
and may I in your truth abide,
    today, O Lord, today.

Move me to seek and do your will,
    today, O Lord, today,
that I may be your servant still,
    today, O Lord, today.

An Ordination Prayer[28]

Almighty God, renew each day
     that faith I once could claim,
when from the depths within my soul
     I heard you speak my name.
O wondrous thought that you should call
     a sinner such as I!
Grant me in Christ the strength to serve
     in this your calling high.

Embolden me by your own will
     to play the prophet's part,
to speak your word with fearless tongue
     yet meek and humble heart.
Instill me with a holy zeal;
     pour out your grace on me;
and let your Spirit fill my life,
     that I your priest may be.

A patient heart I pray to own,
     an attitude of love,
a scornless eye that ne'er disdains
     but rests on you above.
Yet gird me now to meet the world,
     to wield the two-edged sword,
and witness to the truth divine
     that Jesus Christ is Lord!

It's Not In The Bible[29]

"The Lord helps those who help themselves."
 That sounds all right to me.
But if I search the Bible text,
 that line I do not see.

And if I think about it more,
 those words don't say it all.
For God helps those who trust God but
 can't help themselves at all!

Faith, Hope, And Love[30]

There is no faith which knows not faith in God.
       'Tis folly that we trust in worldly things.
For as the weary paths of life we plod,
       whence else can come the comfort Jesus brings?

There is no hope save that we have in him.
       Our feeble striving — is it not in vain?
What solace can we find in fortune's whim,
       when death waits but to mock our earthly gain?

There is no love to match the love of God.
       Can human hearts escape the stain of pride?
Humility gets but a passing nod,
       until we love the one who for us died.

Let us in faith and hope and love abide,
       and strive to live according to God's plan,
all selfish goals, unworthy aims denied,
       for through the living Christ in us we can!

The Master Builder[31]

Who builds the house will labor but in vain,
  unless the Master Builder is the Lord.
Our worldly schemes and ventures wax and wane,
  but God-like effort knows its own reward.

What if our best precautions never cease?
  It is the Lord who must the vigil keep.
And when in faith we sow the seeds of peace,
  the Lord will bless the harvest that we reap.

What if we early rise or late retire,
  to sweat in anxious toil and struggle deep?
They know that labor constant in God's hire:
  God gives to the beloved while they sleep.

Come, Lord, our every thought and deed do guide.
  Our lives are meaningless apart from thee.
Deliver us from self-sufficient pride,
  and let thy face before us ever be.

How Long, O Lord?[32]

How long, O Lord, how long, how long
      before my troubles go?
How long, O Lord, how long it seems
      that I have suffered so!

How long, O Lord, how long, how long
      must sorrow take its toll?
How long, O Lord, how long must I
      bear this pain in my soul?

How long, O Lord, how long, how long
      I've wondered if you knew
how long, O Lord, how long I have
      endured this cross for you.

How long, O Lord, how long, how long,
      before my eyes will see
how long, O Lord, how long, how long
      you have put up with me!

Roller Coaster Ride[33]

Faith is a roller coaster ride for clergy, clerks, or clowns.
>The best disciples, old and new, have had their ups and
downs.

The psalmist and the prophets had their moments of despair,
>and even Jesus, on the cross, had doubts that God was
there.

When faith is riding on the ridge, it shows in word and deed,
>for mountains move if faith is but a grain of mustard
seed.

It's not that we *make* miracles by willing to believe;
>faith's not a work but God's free gift that we by grace
receive.

That thought should keep us humble, when we're feeling strong
and tall.
>The higher up the heights we climb, the farther we can
fall!

As autumn leads to winter's snows and nighttime follows day,
>faith does not always sail the crest nor on the summit
stay,

but sometimes plummets down the steeps with such breathtaking
speed,
>that roller coaster riders should this warning hear and
heed.

Yet when the coaster car is at the bottom of the slope,
>the peaks of faith loom large and give new impetus to
hope.

Then we recall those moments when our faith in God was sure,
>confirmed by truth, sustained by love, we find we can
endure

the ups and downs of faith. Indeed, we now can even say
>without the lows there'd be no highs, without the night
no day.

The ride is always risky, even scary, we'll agree,
>but if we stay inside the car of faith, we're safe. You see,

the roller coaster Maker is the one who takes the toll.
 The car won't ever leave the tracks, if God is in control.
So *re* the roller coaster ride I'll take my own advice
 and hang on tight until the end, no matter what the price.
For when the ride is over and the ups and downs are through,
 I hope to be with God — and all the other riders, too!

Not Of But In The World[34]

Out of the world,
out of the world,
out of the world we come.
Called by the Lord of heaven and earth,
called from above to a second birth,
out of the world we come.

Into the world,
into the world,
into the world we go.
Sent by the One who came from above,
sent in the name of the Lord of love,
into the world we go.

Not of the world,
not of the world,
not of the world are we.
One with the Christ whose name we now bear,
one with each person whose faith we share,
not of the world are we.

Out of the world,
into the world,
not of the world, we say.
Serving the Lord who sends us there
serving the world because we care,
out of the world,
into the world,
not of the world, we pray.

Do You Really Believe?

They were there to learn how to share their faith.
My host had opened with a Bible text
and a brief prayer, followed by a hymn,
which they sang with zest, a few announcements,
and then his most kind introduction of
yours truly, the morning workshop leader.
I began by asking the question which
I have often asked of church groups like this:
"How many of you who have come today
believe in God?" Their reaction was quite
typical — "amazed" would be a good word
to describe their common reaction to
my question, or better, bewilderment,
as if to say, "You can't be serious!
Of course, we believe in God! Otherwise,
why would we be here?" No one said a word
or even nodded. So I asked again:
"Do you believe in a personal God?
I mean, do you really believe in God?
Raise your hand if you do." They realized
now that I was completely serious.
Simultaneously all raised their hands.
"Wait a minute," I said. "I wonder if you
heard the question? What I am asking you
is this: Do you *really* believe in God?"
The hands went up even faster this time.
"Wait! You didn't hear the question. I ask
again: Do you *really* believe in God?

Have you no doubts at all? Are you sure there's
a *personal* God, a God who listens
when you pray and who answers your prayers?
A God who responds to you, and to whom
you are responsible? A God who knows
your deeds, thoughts, hopes, fears, desires, intentions?
Who demands your complete obedience,
your total loyalty — heart, mind and will?
Who is Creator, Redeemer, and Lord
of the universe and your personal
Lord and Savior? Do you really believe
in a God like that?" They sat motionless
for a moment, and then some hands were raised.
Not every hand went up, and those that did
were raised more hesitatingly this time.
Reality was setting in at last.
After a moment I said, "Let me ask
another question: Does the way you live
reveal that you really believe in God?"
Not one hand was raised.   They sat silently.
"If you answer the question too quickly,"
I went on, "you haven't heard the question!"
That's why I have to think each time I say
that I believe in a personal God,
because I know how often my actions
deny my words. Even so, I can say,
with all my heart and soul, and so could they,
"I know that I *really* believe in God!"
To say that, does not mean I have no doubts
or that I'll never do something for which

I'm sorry or ashamed. To say that I
believe is not to claim that I've arrived.
I'm still struggling to be faithful, like the
man who said to Jesus, "I believe; help
my unbelief." That's why I'll always think,
before I raise my hand — and so will they!

The Lord Willing . . .

"Do not boast about tomorrow;
>you don't know what it may bring."
That's the proverb writer's warning.
>So, too, James says the same thing,
when he cautions in his letter
>those who are inclined to say
they'll do this or that tomorrow,
>not to boast of it today.
"What is life?" asks James profoundly.
>"You will vanish like a mist!
All such arrogance is evil.
>If the Lord wills, you exist!"
Therefore we should say "God willing,"
>when we say what we will do;
God who rules the past and present
>is Lord of the future, too.

God is a faith assumption. I can't prove God is there;
   but if I didn't have faith, life would be hard to bear.
I cannot prove to others what I believe is true;
   but those who say there's no God have their assumptions,
   too.
I wish all nonbelievers could understand that fact.
   Then maybe they would state their polemics with more tact.
Whatever our beliefs are, we can share faith, I've found.
   Confessing our assumptions, we stand on common ground.
Then dialogue can take place, if people really care
   and listen to each other. That's what it means to share.

It Means What It Means[38]

Oh, the Bible is a challenge to the mind, to the mind;
     it's a challenge to the mind and to the heart.
If you listen to the Spirit, when you read it, you will find
     that to take it word for word is not too smart.
For it doesn't always mean just what it says, what it says,
     but the Bible always means just what it means.
Any person who can read it can tell others what it says,
     but the test is to interpret what it means!
So to quote a Scripture passage may not be the wisest way,
     if the context of the passage isn't clear.
Any text without a context is a proof text, as they say,
     That's what's wrong with some theology we hear!

God Has Given Us The Word[39]

God has given us the word,
       and the crucial question is,
What in Christ's name have we done
       with the gospel that was his?

God has given us the word,
       and we really ought to be
better stewards than we are
       of that holy mystery.

God has given us the word,
       and we ought to sow the seed
in the minds and hearts of all,
       for it speaks to human need.

God has given us the word
       not to keep it to ourselves,
and our Bibles ought to be
       in our hands, not on the shelves!

Am I Forgiven?[40]

Sometimes I get discouraged,
      and feel somewhat depressed,
when in my honest moments
      my sins I have confessed.
I can't believe that God will
      forgive the likes of me.
But then the Holy Spirit
      by grace helps me to see
that if we are expected
      our neighbors to forgive,
when they have sinned against us,
      as long as we may live,
will we not be forgiven
      through Jesus Christ, God's Son,
when we are truly sorry
      for what we may have done?
My problem with forgiveness
      reveals my lack of trust.
Can I accept God's mercy?
      By grace I can — I must!

The Gift Of Faith[41]

Faith, we say, is a gift.
If so, it must be true
that faith is not something
I can make myself have.
Rather, faith is something
that I find myself with.
I must depend on God
for the faith to go on
believing in the God
I say I believe in,
who is the Author and
Finisher of my faith.

The Devil You Say!

Who's that calculating creature with the cold and shifty eyes?
> Don't be fooled by what he's wearing; it's the devil in
> disguise!

He pretends that he has only your best interests in his heart,
> but he'll tempt you to do something that will tear your life
> apart.

It's no wonder he is known as the Deceiver, for although
> he is called the Prince of Darkness, he is roving to and fro

in a garb that makes you think he is a messenger of light.
> He beguiles you into thinking everything that's wrong is
> right.

Like a roaring lion, always seeking someone to devour,
> he is ready to entrap you any place and any hour.

If you bargain with the Tempter, swift disaster you will see.
> But resist the devil and, the Bible tells us, he will flee!

Don't relax, though, for the Crafty One is never far away.
> He is lurking in the wings 'til he returns another day.

When your doubt of the existence of the devil's power climbs,
> just remember, you have wrestled with him many, many
> times!

Faith And Doubt[43]

I could never figure out
why some people always doubt.
Things that others can affirm
always seem to make them squirm.
Then one day I realized
my concern was ill-advised.
For I came to understand
faith and doubt go hand in hand.
Knowledge is what we should call
faith that knows no doubt at all.
When at last my doubts I faced,
and confessed my faith was based
on the grace of God alone,
then I knew that I had grown
stronger than I was before,
when I was so blindly sure.

Now Is The Time![44]

Christ doesn't call disciples to join him just in name,
  for "nominal" and "faithful" are not at all the same.
To be a faithful witness means following today,
  but many part-time Christians deny him by delay.
All such procrastination, the Lord will disallow.
  The time to follow Jesus is not sometime but now!
Some say that maybe one day they'll make the sacrifice.
  They're like the rich young ruler, who wouldn't pay the price.
They think they have a lifetime to take the holy vow.
  The time for that decision is not someday but now.
It's not when we are ready; it's not just now and then.
  We cannot pick our moments; Christ's call determines when.
To say "I'll do it later" is really to say "No,"
  and all our lame excuses our sinful nature show.
When Christ calls for disciples to put hands to the plow,
  the time is not tomorrow. The time is always now!

A Child's Faith[45]

We're happy that our little grandson Gray
enjoys the times he spends the night with us.
Because he loves the bedtime games we play,
he always goes to bed without a fuss.
Indeed, he bounces up the stairs with joy,
anticipating a "Good night" routine
well calculated to delight a boy
who knows his lines in this well-practiced scene.
So when we've finished all the games once more,
I say, "I think it's time to go to sleep."
And then I make a move toward the door.
But Gray, who knows just what to say to keep
me there, reminds me that I haven't yet
told him a story. "What about?" I ask.
He knows just what reply will always get
me to remain: " 'bout Jesus!" That's a task
he knows I can't refuse. And so I smile
and take my seat again upon his bed.
Then, after I have thought a little while,
about the many things that I have said,
in all the stories I've already told
about the love of Jesus for us all,
I try to talk in words a six-year-old
will understand and later on recall.
One night, when I had told how Jesus had

raised Lazarus, his good friend, from the dead,
I thought, "How can I help this little lad
to deal with such a concept in his head?"
The two of us were soon deeply engrossed
in theological discussion. Gray
was listening intently, and was most
intrigued by everything I had to say
about how even though we cannot see
the Christ, we still can love him as a Friend,
unseen, but real. It is a mystery
a six-year-old would hardly comprehend,
one might have thought. "Gray, can you understand?"
He nodded, as I went on to explain.
"He's always here in spirit, and his hand
is reaching out to heal when we're in pain.
Wherever you may go, you can be glad
he'll be there when you need him. And if you
should ever do something you know is bad,
he will forgive you, if you ask him to,
because he loves you, Gray, and what is more
he'll be your Friend forever! Even when
you die, you can be absolutely sure
that you will be with him in heaven." Then,
I asked Gray what he thought of what I'd said,
as I stood up to go turn out the light.
My grandson, who was lying in the bed,
was wiggling with furious delight!

No wonder Jesus wants us all to turn
and be like little children in our praise.
For what we lukewarm Christians need to learn
is childlike trust and joy in Christ — like Gray's!

Prodigal Parallel[46]

My brother Herb was seventeen, when he one day in May
    got up at dawn, loaded his car, and quietly drove away.
He left a note to tell our parents not to worry, for
    he'd make a fortune and not be a burden any more.
Before that morning I had never seen my father cry.

    The news hit both my parents like a ton of bricks, and I,
a twelve-year-old, did not know what to think, or say, or do,
    for why my brother would run off like that nobody knew.
My brother's disappearance was reported right away.

    Police were searching everywhere throughout the U. S. A.
My father blamed himself, because he felt that he had failed.

    It was a mystery in view of all that it entailed,
for as an intellectual my brother had few peers.

    He'd sparkled at Johns Hopkins University three years,
where he was one of the best students they had ever seen.

    He would have graduated at the age of just eighteen.
He might have been too smart for his own good, and maybe
bored.

    There was a fascinating world out there to be explored.
Herb had been difficult to raise, my parents often said;
    no punishment or force could drive a notion from his head.
He scoffed at unexamined rules and hated to be bossed.

    In his rebelliousness he sometimes failed to count the cost.
I, on the other hand, they said, was more obedient.

    I almost never had to suffer any punishment.
My brother thought that I received more love from them than he,
    but they'd spent far more raising Herb than they had spent
    on me.

They bought him a used car to drive to Hopkins every day,
    and that's the vehicle he used to make his getaway.
He'd told no one at all his plans, and when someone at last
    located him in New Orleans, some seven months had passed.
They found him in a frat house living under a false name,
    deeply in debt, rcmorseful, and holding himself to blame.
He'd sold his car, hocked all his books, and had nowhere to turn,
    and all the grand illusions of the fortune he would earn
had been shipwrecked upon the reef of grim reality.
    Embarrassed and ashamed, he yearned to see his family.
My parents were elated and relieved, to say the least,
    for every day that Herb was gone their worry had increased.
And now they couldn't wait to have their son back home again.
    They hadn't been so happy since I can't remember when.
My father wired Herb a large sum to pay off all his debts.
    It was a sacrifice for one paid what a teacher gets.
He also sent Herb money for his lengthy train-trip home.
    No longer was Dad's main concern, "What led my son to
    roam?"
It was three days till Christmas Eve, when Herb walked through
the door.
    I'd never seen my mom and dad rejoice like that before.
My father never asked Herb to explain why he had left,
    or indicated how much he and Mother were bereft
by his departure, or blamed him for their anxiety.
    They simply celebrated his homecoming gratefully,
and I remember feeling some resentment of the fact
    there was no mention of the pain he'd caused them by his
    act.
But I was glad to have my older brother home again,

and we became much closer after both of us were men.
The prodigal was home again, and I, the younger son,
   observe that in the parable it was the older one
who stayed at home, and did his work, and was obedient.
   The younger son did not return till all he had was spent.
He'd squandered his inheritance and wallowed with the pigs.
   How very like the plight of Herb, alias J. R. Diggs.
I learned so much about myself from Jesus' parable.
   I also learned about God's love, "forever flowing full."
I saw my father's aching heart reach out in selfless love
   and welcome home his wayward son, as God has done
   above.
I understand how God relates to those who stick around,
   and why there is such joy in heaven, when the lost is found.

Gethsemane47

I gaze across the ages to
    a garden of the past,
where shadows of Gethsemane
    their spectral spell now cast,

and through the window of my soul
    into the darkness stare,
until the starry sky reveals
    the ghostly figures there.

As fantasy takes form and shape
    the scene becomes more clear.
It is the Master's face I see,
    and those of others near.

I watch him kneeling, deep in prayer,
    close by three sleeping friends.
How could they all forsake the one
    on whom their life depends?

His sweat appears like drops of blood —
    the Passion has begun!
"Remove this bitter cup," he prays,
    "but let thy will be done."

I hear one call him "Master," then
    betray him with a kiss.
Did ever friend betray a friend
    in such a way as this?

Another who has called him "Lord,"
    and boldly said "I can!"
Will soon deny him with a curse:
    "I do not know the man!"

I look with shame upon the twelve;
    they fail to meet the test.
I know that I for one would not
    forsake him like the rest.

No traitor nor betrayer I,
    nor one who'd flee his call.
Could I but speak, could they but hear,
    I'd castigate them all!

Within the olive shadows yet
    one face remains obscure.
I strain to catch a closer look.
    It must be John, for sure.

But he whom Jesus loved the most
    is running fast away!

Not even John (if it be John)
  is brave enough to stay.

To verify my guess I hold
  my dream-made lantern high,
And phantom flame on fleeing form
  reveals that it is I!

One In Christ[48]

The love of Christ transcends all gaps
    of race, or class, or clan.
If church folk cannot demonstrate
    the love of Christ, who can?

The hurting world must see and hear
    the Christian gospel still.
If church folk will not share the news
    of Jesus' love, who will?

Endnotes

1 John 16:27, " 'For the Father himself loves you, because you have loved me and have believed that I came from the Father.' "

2 Galatians 5:13, "For you were called to freedom. . ."; John 8:32, "And the truth will make you free."

3 Proverbs 18:24, "There are friends who pretend to be friends, but there is a friend who sticks closer than a brother"; John 15:12-17, ". . . You are my friends if you do what I command you. . . ."

4 Luke 4:16-30, "And he came to Nazareth, where he had been brought up. . . ."

5 Galatians 3:28, "There is neither Jew nor Greek, there is neither slave nor free, there is neither male nor female; for you are all one in Christ Jesus."

6 Acts 13:41, "Behold, you scoffers, and wonder, and perish; for I do a deed in your days."

7 Romans 7:15, "I do not understand my own actions. For I do not do what I want, but I do the very thing I hate."

8 Luke 23:26, "And as they led him away, they seized one Simon of Cyrene, who was coming in from the country, and laid on him the cross, to carry it behind Jesus."

9 Luke 2:8-14, ". . . 'And this will be a sign for you: you will find a babe wrapped in swaddling cloths and lying in a manger' . . . ."

10 This poem and the previous one were used as Christmas messages by a religious greeting card company.

11 1 Corinthians 15:10, "But by the grace of God I am what I am."

12 John 7:5, "For even his brothers did not believe in him."

13 Genesis 1:3, "And God said, 'Let there be light'; and there was light."

14 Luke 2:13, "And suddenly there was with the angel a multitude of the heavenly host praising God. . . ."

15 John 6:44, "No one can come to me unless drawn by the Father who sent me." This poem first appeared in my book, *The Pastor-Evangelist In The Parish* (Westminster/John Knox Press, 1990), pp. 123-124.

16 Our son Ricky died early in the morning on the opening day of my first year in seminary. Many have said that the experience of losing a child is one from which a loving parent never fully recovers. I would agree if by that they mean one never totally forgets the sorrow of such a tragic loss. Nor should one forget. But one learns to live with that memory, which even years later can be poignantly evoked by the unexpected occurrence of something that triggers the recall. For many years I wanted to put my feelings of that day into words, but every attempt failed. Perhaps I needed more distance from the event itself. The inspiration finally came a few years ago, and this poem is the result. I felt at the time it was a gift of the God who saw us through that experience and who alone knows what I was feeling that night, and who understands what I wanted and needed to say. The title of the poem refers to the opening convocation in the chapel that evening.

17 Job 1:1, "There was a man in the land of Uz, whose name was Job; and that man was blameless and upright, one who feared God, and turned away from evil."

18 Proverbs 23:18, "Surely there is a future, and your hope will not be cut off."

19 Luke 17:17, "Then said Jesus, 'Were not ten cleansed? Where are the nine?' "

20 Mark 1:7, "After me comes he who is mightier than I, the thong of whose sandals I am not worthy to stoop down and untie."

21 Hebrews 4:15, ". . . one who in every respect has been tempted as we are, yet without sinning."

22 1 Peter 2:21, "For to this you have been called, because Christ also suffered for you, leaving you an example, that you should follow in his steps."

23 Romans 7:19, "For I do not do the good I want, but the evil I do not want is what I do."

24 Romans 8:28, "We know that in everything God works for good with those who love God, who are called according to God's purpose."

25 Isaiah 47:10a, "You felt secure in your wickedness, you said, 'No one sees me.' "

26 John 9:25b, "One thing I know, that though I was blind, now I see."

27 Luke 18:1, "And he told them a parable, to the effect that they ought always to pray and not lose heart."

28 John 15:16, " 'You did not choose me, but I chose you and appointed you that you should go and bear fruit and that your fruit should abide. . . .' "

29 2 Corinthians 12:10, "For the sake of Christ, then, I am content with weaknesses, insults, hardships, persecutions, and calamities; for when I am weak, then I am strong."

30 1 Corinthians 13:13, "So faith, hope, love abide, these three; but the greatest of these is love."

31 Psalm 127:1-2, "Unless the Lord builds the house, those who build it labor in vain. Unless the Lord watches over the city, the watchman stays awake in vain. It is vain that you rise up early and go late to rest, eating the bread of anxious toil; for he gives to his beloved sleep."

32 Psalm 13:1, "How long, O Lord? Wilt thou forget me for-ever?"

33 2 Corinthians 13:5, "Examine yourselves, to see whether you are holding to your faith." This poem first appeared in my book, *The Pastor As Evangelist* (Westminster Press, 1984), pp. 74-75.

34 John 17:6, 16, 18, " . . . whom thou gavest me out of the world. . . They are not of the world. . . So I have sent them into the world."

35 Mark 9:24, "Immediately the father of the child cried out and said, 'I believe; help my unbelief!' "

36 Proverbs 27:1, "Do not boast about tomorrow, for you do not know what a day may bring forth"; James 4:13-15, "Come now, you who say, 'Today or tomorrow we will go into such and such a town and spend a year there and trade and get gain'; whereas you do not know about tomorrow. . . ."

37 Hebrews 11:1, "Now faith is the assurance of things hoped for, the conviction of things not seen."

38 Acts 8:30-31, "So Philip ran to him, and heard him reading Isaiah the prophet, and asked, 'Do you understand what you are reading?' And he said, 'How can I, unless some one guides me?' "

[39] John 17:8, " 'For I have given them the words which thou gavest me, and they have received them and know in truth that I came from thee.' "

[40] 1 John 1:9, "If we confess our sins, he is faithful and just, and will forgive our sins and cleanse us from all unrighteousness"; Matthew 18:21-22, "Then Peter came up and said to him, 'Lord, how often shall my brother sin against me, and I forgive him? As many as seven times?' Jesus said to him, 'I do not say to you seven times, but seventy times seven.' "

[41] Ephesians 2:8, "For by grace you have been saved through faith; and this is not your own doing, it is the gift of God."

[42] 2 Corinthians 11:14, ". . . For even Satan disguises himself as an angel of light."

[43] Mark 9:24, "Immediately the father of the child cried out and said, 'I believe; help my unbelief.' "

[44] John 7:6b, " '. . . but your time is always here.' "

[45] Matthew 18:3, "Truly, I say to you, unless you turn and become like children, you will never enter the kingdom of heaven."

[46] Luke 15:11-32, "Then Jesus said, 'There was a man who had two sons. . . .' "

[47] Matthew 26:36-56, "Then Jesus went with them to a place called Gethsemane."

[48] Galatians 3:28, "There is neither Jew nor Greek, there is neither slave nor free, there is neither male nor female; for you are all one in Christ Jesus."

Index Of First Lines

Topical Index